Tom Sawyer
COLORING BOOK

Mark Twain

Adapted by
Bob Blaisdell

Illustrated by
Jane Wright

DOVER PUBLICATIONS, INC.
Mineola, New York

Bibliographical Note

Tom Sawyer Coloring Book is a new work, first published by Dover Publications, Inc., in 2001.

DOVER *Pictorial Archive* SERIES

International Standard Book Number: 0-486-41672-0

Manufactured in the United States of America
Dover Publications, Inc., 31 East 2nd Street, Mineola, N.Y. 11501

"Tom!"

No answer.

"What's wrong with that boy, I wonder? You, TOM!"

No answer. The old lady pulled her spectacles down and looked over them about the room.

"Well, if I get hold of you I'll—"

There was a slight noise behind her and she turned just in time to seize a small boy by the slack of his jacket and stop his flight.

"There! I might 'a' thought of that closet. Look at your hands. And look at your mouth. What *is* that business?"

"*I* don't know, aunt."

"Well, I know. It's jam—that's what it is. Forty times I've said if you didn't let that jam alone I'd skin you. Hand me that switch."

The switch hovered in the air above the boy—the peril was near—

"My! Look behind you, aunt!"

The old lady whirled round, and snatched her skirts out of danger. The lad fled, instantly, scrambled up the high board fence, and disappeared over it.

His aunt Polly stood surprised a moment, and then broke into a gentle laugh.

"Hang the boy, can't I never learn anything? Ain't he played me tricks enough like that for me to be looking out for him by this time? But my goodness, he never plays them alike, two days, and how is a body to know what's coming? He's my own dead sister's boy, poor thing, and I ain't got the heart to lash him, somehow. He'll play hooky this afternoon, and I'll be obliged to make him work, tomorrow, to punish him."

When Saturday morning came, Tom appeared on the sidewalk with a bucket of whitewash and a long-handled brush. He surveyed the fence, and all gladness left him and a deep sadness settled down upon his spirit. Thirty yards of board fence nine feet high. Sighing he dipped his brush and passed it along the topmost plank; repeated the operation; did it again; compared the tiny whitewashed streak with the far-reaching country of the unwhitewashed fence, and sat down on a tree-box discouraged.

He began to think of the fun he had planned for this day, and his sorrows increased. Soon the boys would come tripping along on all sorts of wonderful outings, and they would make a world of fun of him for having to work. And then inspiration burst upon him!

He took up his brush and went calmly to work. Ben Rogers came in sight soon—the very boy, of all boys, whose teasing he had been dreading. Ben was eating an apple.

Tom went on whitewashing—paid no attention to Ben. The boy stared a moment and then said: "Hi-*yi! You're* up a stump, ain't you!"

No answer. Tom looked over his last touch with the eye of an artist, then he gave his brush another gentle sweep and looked over the result, as before. Ben went up alongside of him. Tom's mouth watered for the apple, but he stuck to his work. Ben said, "Hello, old chap, you got to work, hey?"

Tom wheeled suddenly and said, "Why, it's you, Ben! I warn't noticing."

"*Say*—I'm going in a-swimming, *I* am. Don't you wish you could? But of course you'd druther *work*—wouldn't you?"

Tom looked at the boy a bit, and said, "What do you call work?"

"Why, ain't *that* work?"

Tom began again his whitewashing, and answered, "Well, maybe it is, and maybe it ain't. All I know is, it suits Tom Sawyer."

"Oh, come now, you don't mean to let on that you *like* it?"

The brush continued to move.

"Like it? Well, I don't see why I oughtn't to like it. Does a boy get a chance to whitewash a fence every day?"

That put the thing in a new light. Ben stopped nibbling his apple. Tom swept his brush daintily back and forth—stepped back to note the effect—added a touch here and there—Ben watching every move and getting more and more interested, more and more pulled in. Soon he said, "Say, Tom, let *me* whitewash a little."

Tom considered, was about to say yes; but he changed his mind: "No—no—I reckon it wouldn't hardly do, Ben. You see, Aunt Polly's awful particular about this fence; it's got to be done very careful; I reckon there ain't one boy in a thousand, maybe two thousand that can do it the way it's got to be done."

"No—is that so? Oh, come now—lemme just try. Only just a little—I'd let *you*, if you was me, Tom."

"Ben, I'd like to, honest Injun; but Aunt Polly—well, Jim wanted to do it, but she wouldn't let him; my brother Sid wanted to do it, and she wouldn't let Sid. Now don't you see how I'm fixed? If you was to tackle this fence and anything was to happen to it—"

"Oh, shucks, I'll be just as careful. Now lemme try. Say—I'll give you the core of my apple."

"Well, here—No, Ben, now don't. I'm afeared—"

"I'll give you *all* of it!"

Tom gave up the brush. While Ben worked and sweated in the sun, Tom sat on a barrel close by, dangled his legs, munched his apple, and planned the trap of more boys. There was no lack of them; they came to jeer, but remained to whitewash. By the time Ben was tired out, Tom had traded the next chance to Billy Fisher for a kite; and when *he* played out, Johnny Miller bought in for a dead rat and a string to swing it with—and so on, and so on, hour after hour. And when the middle of the afternoon came, Tom was literally rolling in wealth. He had besides the things before mentioned, twelve marbles, part of a jew's-harp, a piece of blue bottle glass to look through, a spool, a key that wouldn't unlock anything, a piece of chalk, a glass stopper of a bottle, a tin soldier, a couple of tadpoles, six firecrackers, a kitten with only one eye, a brass doorknob, a dog collar—but no dog—the handle of a knife, four pieces of orange peel, and an old window sash.

He had had a nice, good, idle time all the while—plenty of company—and the fence had three coats of whitewash on it! Tom had discovered a great law of human action, without knowing it—namely, that in order to make a man or a boy want a thing, it is only necessary to make the thing difficult to get.

As Tom went to school Monday morning after breakfast, he came upon the young outcast of the village, Huckleberry Finn, son of the town drunkard. Huckleberry was hated and dreaded by all the mothers of the town, because he was idle and lawless and crude and bad—and because all their children admired him so, and delighted in his company, and wished they dared to be like him. Tom was like the rest of the respectable boys, in that he envied Huckleberry and was under strict orders not to play with him. So he played with him every time he got the chance. Huckleberry was always dressed in the castoff clothes of full-grown men, and they were fluttering and ragged. His hat had a wide crescent torn out of its brim; his coat, when he wore one, hung nearly to his heels and had the rear buttons far down the back; only one suspender supported his pants; the seat of his pants bagged low and contained nothing; the fringed legs dragged in the dirt when not rolled up.

Huckleberry came and went, at his own free will. He slept on doorsteps in fine weather and in empty barrels in wet weather; he did not have to go to school or church, or call anybody master or obey anybody. He could go fishing or swimming when and where he chose, and stay as long as it suited him; nobody forbade him to fight; he could sit up as late as he pleased. He was always the first boy that went barefoot in the spring and the last to put on shoes in the fall. He never had to wash, nor put on clean clothes; he could swear wonderfully. In a word, everything that goes to make life good that boy had. So thought every respectable boy in St. Petersburg.

Tom called out, "Hello, Huckleberry!"

"Hello, yourself, and see how you like it."

"What's that you got?"

"Dead cat."

"Lemme see him, Huck. My, he's pretty stiff. Where'd you get him?"

"Bought him off a boy."

"Say—what is dead cats good for, Huck?"

"Good for? Cure warts with."

"But say—how do you cure 'em with dead cats?"

"Why, you take your cat and go and get in the graveyard 'long about midnight when somebody that was wicked has been buried; and when it's midnight a devil will come, or maybe two or three, but you can't see 'em, you can only hear something like the wind, or maybe hear 'em talk; and when they're taking that fellow away, you heave your cat after 'em and say,

'Devil follow corpse, cat follow devil, warts follow cat, *I'm* done with ye!' That'll fetch *any* wart."

"Say, Hucky, when you going to try the cat?"

"Tonight. I reckon they'll come after old Hoss Williams tonight."

"Lemme go with you?"

"Of course—if you ain't afeared."

"Afeared! 'Tain't likely."

When Tom reached the little schoolhouse, he hurried in. He hung his hat on a peg and flung himself into his seat. The teacher, sitting in his armchair, was dozing, but the interruption woke him up. "Thomas Sawyer!"

Tom knew that when his name was pronounced in full, it meant trouble.

"Sir!"

"Come up here. Now, sir, why are you late again, as usual?"

Tom was about to lie, when he saw a new pretty girl with yellow hair

that he wanted to show off for. And beside this girl was the only vacant space on the girls' side of the schoolhouse. He instantly said, "I STOPPED TO TALK WITH HUCKLEBERRY FINN."

"Thomas Sawyer, this is the most astounding confession I have ever listened to. Go and sit with the *girls!* And let this be a warning to you."

Tom sat down upon the end of the pine bench next to the girl. When she turned, he whispered, "What's your name?"

"Becky Thatcher. What's yours? Oh, I know. It's Thomas Sawyer."

"That's the name they lick me by. I'm Tom when I'm good. You call me Tom, will you?"

After school they sat together and fell to talking. Tom was swimming with bliss. He said, "Do you love rats?"

"No! I hate them!"

"Well, I do, too—*live* ones. But I mean dead ones, to swing round your head with a string."

"No, I don't care for rats much, anyway. What *I* like is chewing gum."

"Oh, I should say so. I wish I had some now."

"Do you? I've got some. I'll let you chew it awhile, but you must give it back to me."

That was fine, so they chewed it turn about and dangled their legs against a bench.

At half past nine, that night, Tom and Sid were sent to bed, as usual. They said their prayers, and Sid was soon asleep. Tom lay awake and waited. At midnight Tom was dressed and out the window and creeping along the roof of the house on all fours. He jumped to the roof of the woodshed and then to the ground. Huckleberry Finn was there, with his dead cat. The boys moved off and disappeared in the gloom. At the end of half an hour they were wading through the tall grass of the graveyard.

It was a graveyard of the old-fashioned western kind. It was on a hill, about a mile and a half from the village. It had a crazy board fence around it, which leaned inward in places, and outward the rest of the time, but stood upright nowhere. Grass and weeds grew over the whole cemetery. All the old graves were sunken in, there was not a tombstone on the place; round-topped, worm-eaten boards staggered over the graves, leaning for support and finding none.

A faint wind moaned through the trees, and Tom feared it might be the spirits of the dead, complaining of being disturbed. The boys talked little.

They found the new heap of earth they were seeking, and placed themselves within the protection of three great elms that grew in a bunch within a few feet of the grave.

Then they waited in silence for what seemed a long time. Suddenly Tom grabbed his friend's arm and said, "Sh!"

"What is it, Tom?"

"Sh! There 'tis again. Didn't you hear it?"

"Lord, they're coming! They're coming sure. What'll we do?"

"I don't know. Think they'll see us?"

"Oh, Tom, they can see in the dark, same as cats. I wisht I hadn't come."

A sound of voices floated up from the far end of the graveyard. Some figures approached through the gloom, swinging an old-fashioned tin lantern. Huckleberry whispered, "It's the devils, sure enough. Three of 'em! Lordy, Tom, we're goners!—Wait, they're humans! One of 'em's old Muff Potter's voice."

"Say, Huck, I know another o' them voices; it's Injun Joe."

The whispering died out now, for the three men had reached the grave and stood within a few feet of the boys' hiding place.

"Here it is," said the third voice; and the owner of it held the lantern up and revealed young Dr. Robinson.

Potter and Injun Joe were carrying a handbarrow with a rope and couple of shovels on it. They cast down their load and began to open the grave. The doctor put the lantern at the head of the grave and came and sat down with his back against one of the elm trees. He was so close the boys could have touched him.

"Hurry, men!" he said. "The moon might come out at any moment."

They growled in response and went on digging. Finally a spade struck upon the coffin, and within another minute or two the men had pulled it up and out on the ground. They pried off the lid with their shovels, got out the body and dumped it on the ground. The moon came out from behind the clouds and shone on this scene. The corpse was placed on the barrow and covered with a blanket.

"Now the cussed thing's out, Sawbones, and you'll just pay us out another five, or here it stays," said Potter.

"Look here, what does this mean?" said the doctor. "You asked for your pay in advance, and I've paid you."

"Yes, and you done more than that," said Injun Joe, approaching the

doctor, who was now standing. "Five years ago, you drove me away from your father's kitchen one night, when I come to ask for something to eat, and you said I warn't there for any good; and when I swore I'd get even with you if it took a hundred years, your father had me jailed for a vagrant. Did you think I'd forget?" He was threatening the doctor, with his fist in his face, by this time. The doctor struck out suddenly and knocked the ruffian to the ground.

"Here, now, don't you hit my pard!" said Potter, dropping his knife to the ground. The next moment he had grabbed the doctor and they were struggling. Injun Joe sprang to his feet, his eyes flaming, snatched up Potter's knife, and went round and round the fighters, seeking a chance. All at once the doctor flung himself free, picked up the heavy headboard of Williams' grave and knocked Potter down with it—and in the same instant the half-breed saw his chance and drove the knife to the hilt in the young man's breast. The doctor tumbled over and fell partly on Potter, dashing him with his blood. In the same moment the clouds blotted out the scene and the two frightened boys went speeding away in the dark.

They stopped in the old tannery, panting hard.

"Huckleberry," Tom whispered, "what do you reckon'll come of this?"

"If Dr. Robinson dies, I reckon hanging'll come of it."

"Who'll tell? We?"

"What are you talking about? S'pose something happened and Injun Joe didn't hang? Why he'd kill us some time or other, just as dead sure as we're a-laying here. Now, look-a-here, Tom, let's take and swear to one another to keep mum."

Then they separated. When Tom crept in at his bedroom window the night was almost gone. He undressed and fell asleep.

Close upon the hour of noon the whole village was suddenly electrified with the ghastly news. A gory knife had been found close to the murdered man, and it had been recognized by somebody as belonging to Muff Potter.

All the town was drifting toward the graveyard, even Huck and Tom. Poor Muff Potter was caught nearby, and his eyes showed the fear that was upon him. When the sheriff brought him to the site, Potter stood before the murdered man, put his face in his hands and burst into tears.

"I didn't do it, friends," he sobbed, "'pon my word and honor I never done it." He saw Injun Joe there, and exclaimed, "Tell 'em, Joe, tell 'em!"

Then Huckleberry and Tom stood dumb and staring and heard Injun Joe reel off his lying statement that Potter had killed the doctor. Potter was hauled off to jail.

Tom's fearful secret and conscience disturbed his sleep for as much as a week after this. Every day or two, during this time of sorrow, Tom watched his opportunity and went to the little jail window and smuggled any small comforts through to Potter, the "murderer," as he could get hold of.

One of the reasons why Tom's mind finally drifted away from its secret troubles was that it had found a new matter to interest itself about. Becky Thatcher had stopped coming to school. She was ill. What if she should die? The charm of life was gone.

Finally, one morning at school, Becky passed in at the gate, and Tom's heart gave a great bound. The next instant he was "going on"; yelling, laughing, chasing boys, throwing handsprings, standing on his head—keeping an eye out all the while, to see if Becky was noticing. But she never looked. Could it be possible that she was not aware that he was there? He went closer; came war-whooping around, snatched a boy's cap, hurled it to the roof of the schoolhouse, broke through a group of boys, tumbling them in every direction, and fell sprawling, himself, under Becky's nose, almost upsetting her—and she turned, with her nose in the air, and he heard her say: "Mf! some people think they're smart—always showing off!"

Tom's mind was made up now. He was a forsaken, friendless boy, he said; nobody loved him; when they found out what they had driven him to, perhaps they would be sorry.

By this time he was far down Meadow Lane, away from school. Just at this point he met his soul's sworn comrade, Joe Harper. Tom, wiping his eyes with his sleeve, began to blubber out something about escaping from hard usage and lack of sympathy at home by roaming abroad into the great world never to return.

It happened that Joe had come to Tom to declare such a thing himself. Joe's mother had whipped him for drinking some cream; it was plain that she was tired of him and wished him to go.

As the two boys walked along, they began to lay their plans. Joe was for being a hermit, and living on crusts of bread in a remote cave; but after listening to Tom, he agreed that there were some advantages about a life of crime, and so he went along with becoming a pirate.

Three miles below St. Petersburg, at a point where the Mississippi River was a trifle over a mile wide, there was a long, narrow, wooded island. No one lived there; it lay far over toward the farther shore, near a dense forest. So Jackson's Island was chosen as their pirate camp. Then they hunted for Huckleberry Finn, and he agreed to join them. They separated to meet at a lonely spot two miles above the village at the favorite hour—which was midnight. There was a small log raft there which they meant to capture. Each would bring hooks and lines, and such food as he could steal.

About midnight the boys met, found the raft and shoved off. The raft drew beyond the middle of the river; the boys pointed her head right and then lay on their oars. Hardly a word was said during the next three-quarters of an hour. About two o'clock in the morning the raft grounded on a sand bar two hundred yards above the head of Jackson's Island, and they waded back and forth until they had moved their cargo onto the island.

They built a fire against the side of a great log twenty or thirty steps within the dark depths of the forest, and then cooked up some bacon in the frying pan for supper, and used up half of the corn pone stock they

had brought. It seemed glorious to be feasting far from the haunts of men, and they said they would never return to civilization.

"Ain't it great?" said Joe.

"It's the best," said Tom. "What would the boys say if they could see us?"

"Say? Well, they'd just die to be here—hey, Hucky!"

"I reckon so," said Huckleberry. "Anyways, *I'm* suited. I don't want nothing better'n this."

"It's just the life for me," said Tom. "You don't have to get up, mornings, and you don't have to go to school, and wash, and all that blame foolishness. You see a pirate don't have to do *anything,* Joe, when he's ashore, but a hermit *he* has to be praying considerable, and then he don't have any fun, anyway, all by himself that way."

"Oh, yes, that's so," said Joe. "But I hadn't thought much about it, you know. I'd a good deal rather be a pirate, now that I've tried it."

Gradually their talk died out and sleepiness began to steal upon them.

When Tom awoke in the morning, he wondered where he was. Then he remembered. It was the cool gray dawn, and there was a beautiful feeling of peace in the woods. Tom stirred up the other pirates, and in a minute or two they were stripped and chasing after and tumbling over each other in the shallow water of the white sand bar. They felt no longing for the little village sleeping in the distance beyond the river. A current or rise in the river had carried off their raft, but they were pleased, since its going was something like burning the bridge between them and civilization.

After playing and swimming all day, the boys began to notice a strange sound in the distance. There was a long silence, then a deep boom came floating down out of the distance.

"'Tain't thunder," said Huckleberry.

They sprang to their feet and hurried to the shore toward the town. They parted the bushes on the bank and peered out over the water. The little steam ferryboat was about a mile below the village, drifting with the current. There were a great many rowboats in the neighborhood of the ferryboat, but the boys could not figure out what the men in them were doing. Soon a great jet of white smoke burst from the ferryboat's side, and as it expanded and rose in a lazy cloud, that same dull boom came to the listeners again.

"I know now!" exclaimed Tom. "Somebody's drownded!"

"That's it!" said Huck. "They done that last summer, when Bill Turner got drownded; they shoot a cannon over the water, and that makes him come up to the top."

"By jings, I wish I was over there, now," said Joe.

"I do too," said Huck. "I'd give heaps to know who it is."

"Boys," said Tom, "I know who's drownded—it's us!"

They felt like heroes in an instant. Here was a great triumph; they were missed; they were mourned; hearts were breaking; and best of all, the dead boys were the talk of the whole town, and the envy of all the boys. This was fine. It was worth while to be a pirate.

As twilight drew on, the ferryboat went back and the rowboats disappeared. The pirates returned to their camp. They were jubilant with their new fame and the great trouble they were making. They caught fish, cooked supper and ate, and then fell to guessing at what the village was thinking and saying about them. But when the shadows of night closed them in, they gradually stopped talking, and sat gazing into the fire. The

excitement was gone now, and Tom and Joe could not keep back thoughts of certain persons at home who were not enjoying this fine frolic as much as they were. They grew troubled and unhappy; a sigh or two escaped.

As the night deepened, Huck began to nod, and soon to snore. Joe followed next. Tom lay upon his elbow for some time, watching the two. At last he got up. Then he tiptoed his way among the trees till he felt that he was out of hearing, and broke into a keen run in the direction of the sand bar.

A few minutes later Tom was wading toward the shore. Before the depth reached his middle he was halfway over; the current would permit no more wading, now, so he swam the remaining hundred yards. He went through the woods, following the shore. Shortly before ten o'clock he came out into an open place near the village. He flew along alleys, and shortly found himself at his aunt's back fence. He climbed over and looked in at the sitting-room window, for a light was burning there. There sat Aunt Polly, Sid, Mary, and Joe Harper's mother, grouped together,

talking. They were by the bed, and the bed was between them and the door. Tom went to the door and began to softly lift the latch; then he pressed gently, and the door yielded a crack; he continued pushing, and quaking every time it creaked, till he judged he might squeeze through on his knees.

"What makes the candle blow so?" said Aunt Polly. "Why, that door's open, I believe. Go 'long and shut it, Sid."

Tom disappeared under the bed just in time. He then crept to where he could almost touch his aunt's foot.

"But as I was saying," said Aunt Polly, "he warn't *bad,* so to say—only misch*ee*vous. He never meant any harm, and he was the best-hearted boy that ever was"—and she began to cry.

"It was just so with my Joe—always full of his devilment and up to every kind of mischief, but he was just as unselfish and kind as he could be— and laws bless me, to think I went and whipped him for taking that cream, never once recollecting that I threw it out myself because it was sour, and I never to see him again in this world!" And Mrs. Harper sobbed as if her heart would break.

"Oh, Mrs. Harper," said Aunt Polly, "I don't know how to give him up! He was such a comfort to me, although he tormented my old heart out of me, 'most. But he's out of all his troubles now—"

This was too much for the old lady, and she broke entirely down. Tom was snuffling, now, himself. He went on listening, and gathered by odds and ends that it was thought the boys had been drowned mid-channel, since the boys, being good swimmers, would otherwise have escaped to shore. This was Wednesday night. If the bodies continued missing until Sunday, all hope would be given over and the funerals would be preached on that morning.

Mrs. Harper gave a sobbing goodnight and turned to go. Aunt Polly, by herself now, knelt down and prayed for Tom so touchingly, so appealingly, and with such measureless love in her words and her old trembling voice, that Tom was in tears long before she was through.

He had to keep still long after she went to bed, for she kept making brokenhearted sighs from time to time. But at last she was still, only moaning a little in her sleep. Now the boy stole out, rose gradually by her bedside, and stood regarding her. He bent over and kissed her lips, and right away made his exit, latching the door behind him.

He threaded his way back to the shore opposite the island and swam across and returned to the pirate camp.

For the next couple of days they hunted and played and swam and ran a circus starring three clowns. But by Friday, they were all so homesick they could hardly endure the misery of it.

Joe said, "Oh, boys, let's give it up. I want to go home. It's so lonesome."

"Oh, no, Joe, you'll feel better by and by," said Tom. "Just think of the fishing that's here."

"I don't care for fishing, I want to go home."

"But, Joe, there ain't such another swimming place anywhere."

"Swimming's no good. I don't seem to care for it, somehow, when there ain't anybody to say I shan't go in. I mean to go home."

"Oh, shucks! Baby! You want to see your mother, I reckon."

"Yes, I do want to see my mother—and you would, too, if you had one. I ain't any more baby than you are." And Joe snuffled a little.

"Well, we'll let the crybaby go home to his mother, *won't* we, Huck? *You* like it here, don't you, Huck? We'll stay, won't we?"

Huck said "Y-e-s"—but without any heart in it.

"Go 'long home, Joe," said Tom, "and get laughed at. Oh, you're a nice pirate. Huck and me ain't no crybabies. We'll stay, won't we, Huck?"

Huck now said, "I want to go, too, Tom. It was getting so lonesome anyway, and now it'll be worse. Let's us go, too, Tom."

"I won't! You can all go, if you want to. I mean to stay."

"Tom, I wisht you'd come too. Now you think it over. We'll wait for you when we get to shore."

"Well, you'll wait a blame long time, that's all."

Huck started away, and Tom stood looking after him. He hoped the boys would stop, but they still waded slowly on.

He darted after his comrades, yelling, "Wait! Wait! I want to tell you something!"

They stopped and turned around. When he got to where they were, he began unfolding his secret about Sunday's funeral, and they listened till at last they saw the point he was driving at, and then they set up a war whoop of applause and said it was "splendid!" and said if he had told them at first they wouldn't have started away.

The lads came merrily back and went at their sports again with a will, chattering all the time about Tom's stupendous plan and admiring the genius of it. The next day, Saturday, the boys played Indians all afternoon.

When the Sunday-school hour was finished, the bell began to toll, instead of ringing in the usual way. It was a very quiet Sunday. The villagers began to gather, pausing a moment outside the church to whisper about the sad event. None could remember when the little church had been so full before. When Aunt Polly entered, followed by Sid and Mary, and the Harper family, all in deep black, the congregation rose and stood until the mourners were seated in the front pew.

Then the minister prayed. A moving hymn was sung, and then the sermon followed.

As the service proceeded, the clergyman drew such pictures of the qualities and the great promise of the lost lads that every soul there, thinking he recognized those pictures, felt a pang in remembering that he had seen only faults and flaws in the poor boys. The minister related many a touching event in the lives of the departed, too, which illustrated their sweet, generous natures, and the people could easily see, now, how noble and beautiful those times were. The congregation became more and

more moved, as the sad tale went on, till at last the whole company broke down and joined the weeping mourners in a chorus of sobs, the preacher himself giving way to his feelings and crying in the pulpit.

There was a rustle in the gallery, which nobody noticed; a moment later the church door creaked; the minister raised his streaming eyes above his handkerchief, and stood transfixed! First one and then another pair of eyes followed the minister's, and then almost as one the congregation rose and stared while the three dead boys came marching up the aisle, Tom in the lead, Joe next, and Huck in the rear! They had been hid in the unused gallery listening to their own funeral sermon!

Aunt Polly, Mary, and the Harpers threw themselves upon their restored ones, smothered them with kisses, while poor Huck stood uncomfortable. He started to slink away, but Tom seized him and said: "Aunt Polly, it ain't fair. Somebody's got to be glad to see Huck."

"And so they shall. I'm glad to see him, poor motherless thing!"

Suddenly the minister shouted at the top of his voice: "Praise God from whom all blessings flow—SING!—and put your hearts in it!"

And they did. While the hymn shook the rafters, Tom Sawyer the Pirate looked around him and confessed in his heart that this was the proudest moment of his life.

Vacation came, but the dreadful secret of the murder was a terrible misery to Tom. The murder trial came on in the court. It became the talk of the village immediately and Tom could not get away from it. Every reference to the murder sent a shudder to his heart.

Tom hung about the courtroom, drawn to go in, but forcing himself to stay out. Huck was having the same experience. At the end of the second day the village talk was to the effect that Injun Joe's evidence stood firm and unshaken, and that there was not the slightest question as to what the jury's verdict would be.

Tom was out late that night, doing something, and came to bed through the window. He was in a tremendous state of excitement. It was hours before he got to sleep. All the village flocked to the courthouse the next morning, for this was to be the great day. Potter, pale and haggard, timid and hopeless, was brought into the courtroom, with chains upon him; no less conspicuous there was Injun Joe. When the judge arrived, the sheriff proclaimed the opening of the court.

Now a witness was called who testified that he found Muff Potter washing in the brook, at an early hour of the morning that the murder was discovered. The next witness proved the finding of the knife near the corpse. A third witness swore he had often seen the knife in Potter's possession. Several witnesses talked about Potter's guilty behavior when brought to the scene of the murder.

Every detail of what occurred in the graveyard upon that morning was brought out by believable witnesses, but none of them were cross-examined by Potter's lawyer.

The prosecution now said, "By the oaths of citizens whose simple word is above suspicion, we have fastened this awful crime, beyond all possibility of question, upon the unhappy prisoner. We rest our case."

A groan escaped from poor Potter, and he put his face in his hands and rocked his body softly to and fro. Counsel for the defense rose and said, "Your honor, in our remarks at the opening of this trial, we gave our purpose as proving that our client did this fearful deed while under the influence of too much alcohol. We have changed our mind. We shall not offer that plea." He turned to the clerk and said, "Call Thomas Sawyer!"

A puzzled amazement awoke in every face in the house, not even excepting Potter's. The boy was very scared as he rose and took his place upon the stand.

"Thomas Sawyer, where were you on the seventeenth of June, about the hour of midnight?"

Tom glanced at Injun Joe's iron face and his tongue stopped. The audience listened breathless, but the words refused to come. After a few moments, however, the boy got a little of his strength back, and said: "In the graveyard!"

"A little louder, please. Don't be afraid. You were—"

"In the graveyard."

A savage smile went across Injun Joe's face.

"Were you anywhere near Horse Williams's grave?"

"Yes, sir."

"Speak up—just a trifle louder. How near were you?"

"Near as I am to you."

"Were you hidden, or not?"

"I was hid."

"Where?"

"Behind the elms that's on the edge of the grave."

"Now, my boy, tell us everything that occurred—tell it in your own way—don't skip anything, and don't be afraid."

The climax came when Tom said, "—and the doctor fetched the board around and Muff Potter fell, Injun Joe jumped with the knife and—"

Crash! Quick as lightning the half-breed sprang for a window, tore his way through all opposers, and was gone!

Tom was a glittering hero once more. His name even went into print, for the village paper wrote about him. The village took Muff Potter to its bosom now.

Tom's days were days of splendor, but his nights were seasons of horror. Injun Joe was in all his dreams. Poor Huck was in the same state of terror, for Tom had told the whole story to the lawyer the night before the great day of the trial, and Huck was sore afraid that his share in the business might come out too.

Every day Muff Potter's gratitude made Tom glad he had spoken; but nightly he wished he had sealed up his tongue. Tom felt sure he never could draw a safe breath again until Injun Joe was dead and he had seen the corpse.

The slow days of summer drifted on, and each left behind a slightly lightened weight of fear on Tom.

There comes a time in every boy's life when he has a raging desire to go somewhere and dig for hidden treasure. This desire came upon Tom one day. He stumbled upon Huck, and told Huck about it, and Huck was willing.

"Where'll we dig?" he asked.

"Oh," said Tom, "most anywhere."

"Why, is it hid all around?"

"No, indeed it ain't. It's hid in mighty particular places, Huck—sometimes on islands, sometimes in rotten chests under the end of a limb of an old dead tree, just where the shadow falls at midnight."

"Is it under all of them?"

"How you talk! No!"

"Then how you going to know which one to go for?"

"S'pose we tackle that old dead-limb tree on the hill t'other side of Still-House branch?"

"I'm agreed."

So they got a pick and a shovel, and set out on their three-mile tramp.

When they got there they worked and sweated for half an hour. No result. They toiled another half hour without result. Huck said, "Do they always bury it as deep as this?"

"I reckon we haven't got the right place," said Tom. "Oh, I know what the matter is! What a blamed lot of fools we are! You got to find out where the shadow of the limb falls at midnight, and that's where you dig!"

"Then consound it, we've fooled away all this work for nothing. Well, I'll come around and meow tonight."

"All right."

The boys were there that night, about the appointed time. They marked where the shadow fell, and began to dig. The hole deepened and still deepened. At last Tom said, "It ain't any use, Huck, we're wrong again."

Huck dropped his shovel. "Say, Tom, let's give this place up, and try somewheres else."

"All right, I reckon we better. The haunted house. That's it!"

"Blame it, I don't like haunted houses, Tom. And you know mighty well people don't go about that haunted house in the day nor the night."

"But ghosts don't come around in the daytime, so what's the use of our being afeared?"

"Well, all right. We'll tackle the haunted house tomorrow in the daytime if you say so—but I reckon it's taking chances."

They had started down the hill by this time and took their way homeward through the woods.

In the afternoon the next day the boys arrived at the haunted house. They crept to the door and took a peep. They saw a weed-grown, floorless room, an ancient fireplace, empty windows, a ruinous staircase; and here, there, and everywhere hung cobwebs. They entered, talking in whispers. They wanted to look upstairs. They threw their tools into a corner and made the climb. Up there were the same signs of decay. They were about to go down and begin work when—

"Sh!" said Tom.

"What is it?" whispered Huck.

"They're coming right toward the door."

The boys stretched themselves upon the floor with their eyes to knot-holes in the planking.

Two men entered the house. Each boy said to himself, "There's the old deaf-and-dumb Spaniard that's been about town lately—never saw t'other man before."

"T'other" man was a ragged creature, with nothing very pleasant in his face. The Spaniard was wrapped in a serape; he had bushy white whiskers; long white hair flowed from under his sombrero. When they came in, "t'other" was talking in a low voice. "No," said he, "it's dangerous."

"Dangerous!" grunted the "deaf-and-dumb" Spaniard—to the vast surprise of the boys. "Coward!"

The voice made the boys gasp and quake. It was Injun Joe's!

Injun Joe said, "I'm dead for sleep! It's your turn to watch."

Soon enough, however, both men began to snore.

The boys drew a long, grateful breath. Tom whispered: "Now's our chance—come!" Tom rose slowly and softly, and started. But the first step he made wrung such a hideous creak from the crazy floor that he sank down almost dead with fright.

Now one snore ceased. Injun Joe sat up, stared around and stirred up his comrade with his foot and said, "You're a watchman, ain't you!"

"My! have I been asleep?"

"Oh, partly. It's sunset, nearly time for us to be moving, pard. What'll we do with what little dough we've got left?"

"I don't know—leave it here as we've always done, I reckon. No use to take it away till we start south. Six hundred in silver's something to carry."

"Well—all right—it won't matter to come here once more. We'll just bury it."

"Good idea."

The boys forgot all their fears, all their miseries in an instant. With gloating eyes they watched every movement. Luck! Six hundred dollars was money enough to make half a dozen boys rich! Here was the best sort of treasure hunting—they would not be wondering where to dig!

As Joe dug with his knife, it struck upon something.

"Hello!" said he.

"What is it?" said his comrade.

"It's a box, I believe." He reached his hand in through a hole in the wooden plank and drew it out—"Man, it's money!"

The two men examined the handful of coins. They were gold!

Joe's comrade said, "We'll make quick work of getting the rest of the box out. There's an old rusty pick over in the corner." He ran and brought the boys' pick and shovel. Injun Joe took the pick and unearthed the box.

"Pard," said Injun Joe, "there's thousands of dollars here."

"What'll we do with this—bury it again?"

"Yes."

At this answer Tom and Huck were delighted.

Then Injun Joe declared, "No! by the great sachem, no! I'd nearly forgot. That pick had fresh earth on it. What business has a pick and shovel here? Who brought them here—and where are they gone? What! bury it again and leave them to come and see the ground disturbed? Not exactly. We'll take it to my den."

"You mean Number One?"

"No—Number Two—under the cross. The other place is bad—too common."

"All right. It's nearly dark enough to start."

Shortly afterward they slipped out of the house and moved toward the river with their precious box.

Tom and Huck rose up, weak, and stared after them through the chinks between the logs of the house. Follow? Not they. They were content to get out of the house alive, and take the townward track over the hill.

The next week Tom heard that Judge Thatcher's family had come back to town. Becky was back from vacation! Both Injun Joe and the treasure sank into secondary importance for a moment, and Becky took the chief place in the boy's interest. He saw her, and they had a good time playing with a crowd of their schoolmates. The day was crowned in a fine way: Becky managed to get her mother to name the next day, a Saturday, as a picnic for all her friends.

By eleven o'clock the next morning a giddy company were gathered at Judge Thatcher's, and everything was ready for a start. The children were escorted by young ladies of eighteen and a few young gentlemen. The old steam ferryboat was chartered for the occasion.

Three miles below town the ferryboat stopped at the mouth of a woody hollow and tied up. The crowd swarmed ashore and soon there were shouts and laughter. After the picnic there was a time of resting and chatting in the shade of the spreading oaks. By and by somebody shouted: "Who's ready for the cave?"

Everybody was. Bundles of candles were passed around, and right away there was a general scamper up the hill. The mouth of the cave was up the hillside—an opening shaped like the letter A. Its massive oaken door stood unbarred. Within was a small chamber, chilly as an icehouse, and walled by nature with solid limestone that was dewy with a cold sweat.

The procession of children and young men and women went filing down the steep descent of the main path, the flickering candle lights dimly revealing the lofty walls of rock. McDougal's Cave was a vast labyrinth, a maze of crooked aisles that ran into each other and out again and led nowhere.

The parade moved along the main path some three-quarters of a mile, and then groups and couples began to slip aside into branch avenues. By and by one group after another came straggling back to the mouth of the cave, panting, entirely delighted with the success of the day. They were astonished to find that they had been taking no note of time and that night was about at hand. The ferryboat with her wild passengers pushed into the stream and headed for home.

Meanwhile, Tom and Becky had been left behind. They had visited the familiar wonders of the cave with the rest of the company. Then the hide-and-seek had begun, and Tom and Becky had played along until they got tired of it and wandered down a curving path. Still drifting along and talking, they came to a place where a little stream of water trickled over a ledge. Tom found a steep natural stairway behind it. They started upon their quest to explore further into the cave. They wound this way and that, far down into the secret depths of the cave, and branched off in search of novelties to tell the others about.

They came to a spring in the midst of a cavern, whose walls were supported by many fantastic pillars which had been formed by the joining of great stalactites and stalagmites. Under the roof vast knots of bats had packed themselves together, thousands in a bunch; the lights disturbed the creatures, and they came flocking down by hundreds, squeaking and darting at the candles. Tom seized Becky's hand and hurried her into the first corridor they found; and none too soon, for a bat struck Becky's light out with its wing while she was passing out of the cavern. The bats chased the children a good distance; but Tom and Becky plunged into every new passage they found and at last got rid of the dangerous things. Tom found an underground lake, shortly, and they sat down by it and rested awhile.

Becky said, "It seems ever so long since I heard any of the others."

"Come to think, Becky, we are away down below them—and I don't know how far away north, or south, or east, or whichever way it is. We couldn't hear them here."

"I wonder how long we've been down here, Tom. We better start back."

"Yes, I reckon we better. But if the bats put both our candles out it will be an awful fix. Let's try some other way, so as not to go through there."

"Well, I hope we won't get lost."

But indeed they did get hopelessly lost.

They were finally so weary with hiking through the tunnels and along the underground paths that they lay down and slept. When they woke they walked further and drank some spring water. They were down to their last candle.

Becky said, "They'll miss us and hunt for us!"

"Yes, they will! Certainly they will!"

The children fastened their eyes upon their bit of candle and watched it melt slowly away, and then—the horror of utter darkness! The weary time dragged on; they slept again and awoke famished. Tom believed it must be Tuesday by this time.

Now an idea struck him. There were some side passages near at hand. He took a kite string from his pocket, tied it to a rock, and he and Becky started, Tom in the lead, unwinding the line as he groped along. At the end of twenty steps the corridor ended in a "jumping-off place." Tom got down on his knees and felt below, and then as far around the corner as he could reach with his hands. He made an effort to stretch yet a little farther to the right, and at that moment, not twenty yards away, a human hand, holding up a candle, appeared from behind a rock! Tom lifted up a

glorious shout, and instantly that hand was followed by the body it belonged to—Injun Joe's. Tom could not move. He was happy the next moment to see Joe take to his heels and get himself out of sight. Tom wondered that Joe had not recognized his voice and come over and killed him for testifying against him in court. Tom now got his strength back and returned to Becky. He was careful to keep from her what he had seen. He told her he had only shouted "for luck."

They waited and waited by the spring and had another long sleep. The children awoke tortured with a raging hunger. Tom believed that it must be Wednesday or Thursday or even Friday or Saturday now, and that the search had been given up. He proposed to explore another passage. He felt willing to risk Injun Joe and all other terrors. But Becky was very weak. She said she would wait now, where she was, and die—it would not be long. She told Tom to go with the kite line and explore if he chose.

Tuesday afternoon came and went. The village of St. Petersburg mourned for the lost children. The majority of the cave searchers had given up the quest and gone back to their daily lives, saying it was plain the children could never be found. Mrs. Thatcher was very ill. Aunt Polly had drooped into a settled sadness, and her gray hair had turned almost white.

Away in the middle of the night a wild peal burst from the village bells, and in a moment the streets were swarming with half-dressed people who shouted, "They're found! They're found!" Tin pans and horns were added to the din, and the population moved toward the river and met the children coming in an open carriage drawn by shouting citizens.

Aunt Polly's happiness was complete, and Mrs. Thatcher's as well. Tom lay upon a sofa at Aunt Polly's and told the history of the wonderful adventure and closed with a description of how he left Becky and went on an exploring expedition; how he followed two paths as far as his kite string would reach; how he followed a third to the fullest stretch of the string, and was about to turn back when he glimpsed a far-off speck that looked like daylight; dropped the line and groped toward it, pushed his head and shoulders through a small hole and saw the broad Mississippi rolling by! He told how he went back for Becky and broke the good news and how she almost died with joy when she had groped to where she actually saw the blue speck of daylight; how he pushed his way out at the hole and then helped her out; how they sat there and cried for gladness; how some men came along in a rowboat and Tom hailed them and told them their troubles; how the men didn't believe the wild tale at first, "Because," they said, "you are five miles down the river below the valley the cave is in"— then took them aboard, rowed to a house, gave them supper, made them rest till two or three hours after dark, and then brought them home.

About two weeks after Tom's rescue from the cave, he stopped to see Becky. The judge and some friends set Tom to talking, and someone asked him, as a joke, if he wouldn't like to go to the cave again. Tom said he thought he wouldn't mind it.

The judge said, "Well, there are others just like you, Tom. But nobody will get lost in that cave any more, because I had its big door covered with iron two weeks ago, and triple locked—and I've got the keys."

"Oh, judge, Injun Joe's in the cave!"

Within a few minutes the news had spread, and a dozen rowboats of men were on their way to McDougal's Cave, and the ferryboat, well filled with passengers, soon followed. Tom Sawyer was in the rowboat that brought Judge Thatcher.

When the cave door was unlocked, a sorrowful sight presented itself in the dim twilight of the place. Injun Joe lay stretched upon the ground, dead, with his face close to the crack of the door. Tom was touched, for he knew by his own experience how this wretch had suffered. His pity was moved, but nevertheless he felt a sense of relief and security, now, which showed him how huge a weight of dread had been lying upon him since the day he testified against this bloody-minded outcast.

Injun Joe was buried near the mouth of the cave.

The morning after the funeral Tom took Huck to a private place to have an important talk.

"Huck, that treasure's in the cave!"

"Tom—honest, now—is it fun or true?"

"True, Huck—just as true as I ever I was in my life. Will you go in there with me and help get it out?"

"I bet I will!"

They borrowed a rowboat and got under way at once. When they were several miles down the river, they landed, and Tom showed Huck the hidden entrance.

They entered the hole, Tom in the lead. They toiled their way to the farther end of the tunnel, then tied their kite strings to rocks and moved on. A few steps brought them to the spring. They went on and soon entered and followed Tom's other corridor until they reached the "jumping-off place." The candles showed that it was not really a cliff, but only a steep clay hill twenty or thirty feet high. Tom held his candle high and said, "Huck, look as far around the corner as you can. Do you see that? There—on the big rock over yonder—done with candle-smoke."

"Tom, it's a *cross!*"

"'*Under the cross,*' hey? Right yonder's where I saw Injun Joe poke up his candle!"

"It's luck for us, that cross is," said Huck.

They searched everywhere for the box, and then sat down discouraged. By and by Tom said, "I bet you the money is under the rock!"

Tom's knife was out at once, and he had not dug four inches before he struck wood.

"Hey, Huck!—do you hear that?"

Huck began to dig and scratch now. Some boards were soon uncovered and removed. They had hidden a natural hole which led under the rock. Tom got into this hole and held his candle as far under the rock as he could, but could not see to its bottom. He stooped and passed under the rock. He followed its winding course, first to the right, then to the left, Huck at his heels. Tom turned a short curve and exclaimed, "My goodness, Huck, looky-here!"

It was the treasure box, sure enough, occupying a snug little cavern, along with an empty gunpowder keg, a couple of guns in leather cases, two or three pairs of old moccasins, and a leather belt.

"Got it at last!" said Huck. "My, but we're rich, Tom!"

"Huck, I always reckoned we'd get it. It's just too good to believe, but we have got it, sure!"

They transferred the money from the box into the bags they had brought along, and the boys took it up to the cross rock.

They soon came out into the clump of sumac bushes by the entry hole, looked carefully out, found the coast clear, and were soon lunching in the rowboat. They landed back in the village shortly after dark.

"Now, Huck," said Tom, "we'll hide the money in the loft of the widow's woodshed, and I'll come up in the morning and we'll count it and divide it, and then we'll hunt up a place out in the woods for it where it will be safe."

But just as soon as they had hid the money, a Mr. Jones saw them coming out and asked them to come along with him to the Widow Douglas's drawing room.

The place was grandly lighted, and everybody that was of any importance in the village was there. The Thatchers were there, the Harpers, the Rogerses, Aunt Polly, Sid, Mary, the minister, the editor, and a great many more, and all dressed in their best. The widow received the boys as heartily as anyone could well receive two such looking beings. They were covered with clay and candle grease. Aunt Polly blushed and frowned and shook her head at Tom.

"Come with me, boys," said the Widow Douglas.

She took them to a bedroom and said, "Now wash and dress yourselves. Here are two new suits of clothes—shirts, socks, everything complete. Get into them. We'll wait—come down when you are slicked up enough."

Some minutes later the Widow Douglas's guests were at the supper table, and a dozen children propped up at little side tables in the same room. The widow now announced that she meant to give Huck a home under her roof and have him educated; and that when she could spare the money she would start him in business.

Tom said, "Huck don't need it. Huck's rich. You just wait a minute." Tom ran out of doors. The company looked at each other and at Huck, who was tongue-tied.

"Sid, what ails Tom?" said Aunt Polly. "He—well, there ain't ever any making of that boy out. I never—"

Tom entered, struggling with the weight of his sacks, and Aunt Polly did not finish her sentence. Tom poured the mass of yellow coin upon the table and said, "There—what did I tell you? Half of it's Huck's and half of it's mine!"

The spectacle took the general breath away. All gazed, nobody spoke for a moment. Then there was a call for an explanation. Tom's tale was long, but brimful of interest.

The money was counted. The sum amounted to a little over twelve thousand dollars. The Widow Douglas put Huck's money into a bank account, and Judge Thatcher did the same with Tom's at Aunt Polly's request. Judge Thatcher had a great opinion, now, of Tom. He said that no commonplace boy would ever have got his daughter out of the cave.

Huck Finn's wealth and the fact that he was now under the Widow Douglas's protection introduced him into society. The widow's servants kept him clean and neat, combed and brushed, and they bedded him nightly in fresh sheets. He had to eat with knife and fork; he had to use napkin, cup, and plate; he had to learn his book; he had to go to church; he had to talk so properly that his speech was becoming boring in his mouth.

He bravely bore his miseries three weeks, and then one day turned up missing. For forty-eight hours the widow hunted for him everywhere in great distress. Early the third morning Tom Sawyer wisely went poking among the old empty barrels down behind the abandoned slaughter-house, and in one of them he found Huck. He had slept there; he had just breakfasted upon some stolen odds and ends of food, and was lying down, now, in comfort, with his pipe. He was dirty, uncombed, and wearing the same old rags that had made him so interesting to look at in the days when he was free and happy. Tom told him the trouble he had been causing, and urged him to go home. Huck's face turned sad. He said:

"Don't talk about it, Tom. I've tried it, and it don't work. It ain't for me. The widder's good to me, and friendly; but I can't stand them ways. She makes me git up just at the same time every morning; she makes me wash, they comb me all to thunder; she won't let me sleep in the woodshed; I got to wear them blamed clothes that just smothers me, Tom; they don't seem to let any air git through 'em, somehow; and they're so rotten nice that I can't set down, nor lay down, nor roll around anywhere's; I got to go to church and sweat and sweat—I hate them ornery sermons! I can't ketch a fly in there, I can't chaw. I got to wear shoes all Sunday. The widder eats by a bell; she goes to bed by a bell; she gits up by a bell—everything's so awful reg'lar a body can't stand it."

"Well, everybody does that way, Huck."

"Tom, it don't make no difference. I ain't everybody, and I can't *stand* it. And, besides, that school's going to open, and I'd 'a' had to go to it—well, I wouldn't stand *that*. Looky-here, Tom, being rich ain't what it's cracked up to be. It's just worry and worry. I wouldn't ever got into all this trouble if it hadn't 'a' been for all that money; now you just take my sheer of it along with yourn, and gimme a ten-center sometimes, and you go and beg off for me with the widder."

"Oh, Huck, you know I can't do that. 'Tain't fair. And, besides, if you'll try this thing just a while longer you'll come to like it."

"Like it! No, Tom, I won't be rich, and I won't live in them cussed smothery houses. I like the woods, and the river, and the barrels, and I'll stick to 'em, too. Blame it all!"

"But, Huck, we can't let you into the gang if you ain't respectable, you know."

Huck's joy disappeared. "Can't let me in, Tom? You wouldn't shet me out, would you, Tom?"

"Huck, I wouldn't want to, and I *don't* want to—but what would people say? Why, they'd say, 'Mf! Tom Sawyer's Gang! pretty low characters in it!' They'd mean you, Huck. You wouldn't like that, and I wouldn't."

Huck was silent for a time. Finally he said, "Well, I'll go back to the widder for a month and tackle it and see if I can come to stand it, if you'll let me b'long to the gang, Tom."

"All right, Huck, it's a whiz! Come along, old chap, and I'll ask the widow to let up on you a little."

"Will you, Tom—now will you? That's good. If she'll let up on some of the roughest things, I'll smoke private and cuss private, and crowd through or bust. When you going to start the gang?"

"Oh, right off. We'll get the boys together and have the initiation tonight, maybe."

"Have the which?"

"Have the initiation."

"What's that?"

"It's to swear to stand by one another, and never tell the gang's secrets. And all that swearing's got to be done at midnight, in the lonesomest, awfulest place you can find—a haunted house is the best, but they're all ripped up now."

"Well, midnight's good, anyway, Tom."

"Yes, so it is. And you've got to swear on a coffin, and sign it in blood."

"Now, that's something like! Why, it's a million times bullier than pirating. I'll stick to the widder till I rot, Tom; and if I git to be a reg'lar ripper of a robber, and everybody talking 'bout it, I reckon she'll be proud she brought me in out of the wet."